Disadvantages of internet are less but advantages are more

Introduction:

The internet has transformed the world in many ways, bringing people together from all corners of the globe and making information easily accessible to anyone with an internet connection. While the advantages of the internet are numerous, it would be wrong to assume that it is without its drawbacks. In this essay, we will explore the advantages and disadvantages of the internet and consider whether the benefits outweigh the costs.

Advantages of the Internet:

One of the most significant advantages of the internet is the way it has revolutionized the way we communicate with each other. We can now communicate with people on the other side of the world instantly, through a variety of platforms, such as email, social media, and messaging apps. The internet has also made it possible for people to work from home, which has made it easier for people to balance work and family life.

Another advantage of the internet is the amount of information that is available at our fingertips. Whether you want to learn about a new hobby, research a medical condition, or find out about a historical event, the internet provides access to a wealth of information. The internet has also made it possible for people to access education and training courses that they may not have been able to attend in person.

Disadvantages of the Internet:

While the internet has many advantages, it is important to acknowledge that it also has some disadvantages. One of the most significant disadvantages of the internet is the spread of misinformation. With so much information available, it can be difficult to distinguish between fact and fiction. This has led to the spread of fake news, conspiracy theories, and propaganda, which can have real-world consequences.

Another disadvantage of the internet is the potential for addiction. With social media platforms, online gaming, and other digital distractions, it can be easy to spend hours online without realizing how much time has passed. This can have a negative impact on mental health, social relationships, and productivity.

Conclusion:

In conclusion, while the advantages of the internet are many, it is important to be aware of the potential drawbacks. Misinformation and addiction are just two examples of the challenges that come with living in an increasingly connected world. However, with awareness and responsible use, the benefits of the internet can far outweigh the costs, making it a powerful tool for communication, education, and innovation.

Index

1. **Communication:** The internet has made it possible to communicate with people from all over the world in real-time. Whether it's through email, social media, or video conferencing, the internet has revolutionized the way we interact with others.

2. **Access to information:** The internet provides access to a vast amount of information on a variety of topics. From news to research, the internet has made it easier than ever to learn about anything and everything.

3. **Entertainment:** With streaming services, online gaming, and social media, the internet has made entertainment more accessible and varied than ever before.

4. **Convenience:** The internet has made it possible to shop, bank, and access services online, saving time and effort.

5. **Education:** The internet has made education more accessible and affordable, with online courses and resources available to people around the world.

6. **Networking:** The internet has made it possible to connect with like-minded individuals and build professional and personal networks.

7. **Innovation:** The internet has enabled innovation in a variety of fields, from technology to healthcare, leading to new discoveries and advancements.

8. **Globalization:** The internet has facilitated globalization, allowing businesses and individuals to connect and collaborate on a global scale, leading to greater economic growth and cultural exchange.

Chapter-1

Communication: The internet has made it possible to communicate with people from all over the world in real-time. Whether it's through email, social media, or video conferencing, the internet has revolutionized the way we interact with others

The internet has transformed the way we communicate, enabling us to connect with people from all corners of the world in real-time. From sending emails to video conferencing and social media, the internet has made communication easier, faster and more accessible than ever before.

One of the most significant advantages of the internet is that it has eliminated the barriers of distance and time, allowing people to communicate with each other instantly, regardless of their location. This has opened up a world of opportunities for individuals and businesses alike, enabling them to connect with others across the globe in ways that were previously impossible.

Email is one of the most common forms of online communication, and it has become an essential tool for both personal and professional purposes. It allows us to send messages, documents and files to people all over the world instantly, without the need for postage or waiting for delivery.

Social media has also transformed the way we interact with others. Sites like Facebook, Twitter, and Instagram have made it easy to connect with friends, family and colleagues in real-time, and to share our experiences, thoughts and feelings with others. Social media has also become a powerful tool for businesses, enabling them to engage with customers, promote their products and services, and build brand awareness.

Video conferencing is another significant development in online communication, allowing people to hold face-to-face meetings and discussions from anywhere in the world. Services like Zoom and Skype have become increasingly popular, especially during the COVID-19 pandemic, when many people have had to work and socialize remotely.

However, the internet has also created some challenges and concerns regarding communication. The anonymity of the internet has led to an increase in cyberbullying, online harassment, and hate speech, which can be damaging to individuals and communities. Additionally, the sheer volume of information available online can make it difficult to distinguish between fact and fiction, and to identify reliable sources of information.

In conclusion, the internet has revolutionized the way we communicate, making it easier, faster and more accessible than ever before. From email to social media and video conferencing, the internet has created a world of opportunities for individuals and businesses to connect with others across the globe. However, we must also be aware of the challenges and concerns that come with online communication, and take steps to address them.

Chapter-2

Access to information: The internet provides access to a vast amount of information on a variety of topics. From news to research, the internet has made it easier than ever to learn about anything and everything

The internet has revolutionized the way we access information, providing us with a wealth of knowledge on a vast range of topics. From news and current events to research and academic articles, the internet has made it easier than ever to learn about anything and everything.

One of the most significant advantages of the internet is the access it provides to information. With just a few clicks, we can access a vast amount of information on any topic imaginable. This has transformed the way we learn and research, making it possible to gather information quickly and easily from anywhere in the world.

News is one of the most widely accessed forms of information online, and the internet has become a primary source for staying up-to-date on current events. Online news websites, social media platforms, and blogs provide instant access to breaking news stories from around the world. This has made it easier for people to stay informed and to engage with global events in real-time.

The internet has also made it possible for people to access a vast amount of academic and research-based information. Online databases, digital libraries, and scholarly journals provide access to research articles and publications that were previously only available to a select few. This has opened up a world of knowledge to anyone with an internet connection, providing opportunities for learning and education on a global scale.

The internet has also made it easier for individuals and businesses to access information related to their specific interests and needs. Online forums, blogs, and social media groups allow people to connect with others who share their interests and to exchange information and ideas. This has created new opportunities for collaboration and innovation, allowing people to work together across borders and time zones.

However, the internet also presents some challenges and concerns when it comes to accessing information. The sheer volume of information available online can make it difficult to identify reliable sources of information, and misinformation and fake news can spread rapidly online. Additionally, some people may not have access to the internet, which can limit their ability to access information and participate in the digital world.

In conclusion, the internet has transformed the way we access information, providing us with a wealth of knowledge on a vast range of topics. From news to research, the internet has made it easier than ever to learn about anything and everything. While there are challenges and concerns associated with accessing information online, the benefits of the internet as a tool for learning and education cannot be overstated.

Chapter-3

Entertainment: With streaming services, online gaming, and social media, the internet has made entertainment more accessible and varied than ever before

The internet has revolutionized the entertainment industry, providing access to a vast range of content and experiences that were previously unavailable to many people. With streaming services, online gaming, and social media, the internet has made entertainment more accessible and varied than ever before.

Streaming services like Netflix, Amazon Prime Video, and Disney+ have transformed the way we watch TV shows and movies. These services allow users to watch content on demand, at any time and from any location, without the need for traditional broadcast schedules or physical media. This has provided viewers with greater control over their viewing experience, and has made it easier to discover new content.

Online gaming has also become a major form of entertainment on the internet. With games like Fortnite, Minecraft, and Call of Duty, online gaming has become a global phenomenon, with millions of players from around the world participating in multiplayer games and tournaments. Online gaming has created new opportunities for social interaction, enabling players to connect and collaborate with others from different cultures and backgrounds.

Social media has also become a major source of entertainment on the internet. Sites like Facebook, Instagram, and TikTok provide a platform for sharing and viewing user-generated content, including videos, photos, and memes. This has created a new form of entertainment that is highly interactive and engaging, and has provided opportunities for people to express themselves creatively.

The internet has also created new opportunities for independent creators and artists to share their work with a global audience. YouTube, for example, has become a major platform for online content creators, with millions of videos covering a vast range of topics, from music and comedy to education and activism.

However, the internet also presents some challenges and concerns when it comes to entertainment. The sheer volume of content available online can make it difficult for users to identify quality content, and there are concerns around the impact of online content on mental health and well-being. Additionally, online piracy and copyright infringement remain major issues in the entertainment industry, as does the spread of fake news and disinformation.

In conclusion, the internet has transformed the entertainment industry, providing access to a vast range of content and experiences that were previously unavailable to many people. From streaming services to online gaming and social media, the internet has made entertainment more accessible and varied than ever before. While there are challenges and concerns associated with online entertainment, the benefits of the internet as a tool for entertainment cannot be overstated.

Chapter-4

Convenience: The internet has made it possible to shop, bank, and access services online, saving time and effort

The internet has transformed the way we live our daily lives, providing a vast range of services and resources that make our lives more convenient and efficient. From shopping and banking to accessing services and information, the internet has made it easier than ever to manage our daily tasks and responsibilities.

Online shopping has become a major form of retail, providing consumers with the ability to shop for products from anywhere in the world. E-commerce platforms like Amazon, eBay, and Alibaba have made it possible for consumers to browse and purchase products online, and have streamlined the shopping process, making it more convenient and efficient.

Online banking has also become a major feature of the internet, allowing people to manage their finances from the comfort of their own homes. Online banking platforms provide a range of services, including account management, bill payments, and money transfers, making it easy to manage finances without the need to visit a physical bank branch.

The internet has also made it possible to access a wide range of services online, including healthcare, education, and government services. Telemedicine, for example, enables patients to consult with healthcare professionals remotely, while online education platforms provide access to courses and training from anywhere in the world. Government services like tax filings and passport applications can also be completed online, saving time and effort for both citizens and government officials.

In addition to these services, the internet has also made it easier for people to access information on a wide range of topics. Search engines like Google and Bing allow users to quickly and easily find information on anything from current events to scientific research, while social media platforms enable users to connect with others who share their interests and to exchange information and ideas.

However, the convenience of the internet also presents some challenges and concerns. Cybersecurity and online privacy are major issues in the digital age, with hackers and cybercriminals posing a significant threat to individuals and businesses. Additionally, the rise of online platforms has led to concerns around the impact of technology on society, including issues related to addiction, mental health, and social isolation.

In conclusion, the internet has transformed the way we live our daily lives, providing a vast range of services and resources that make our lives more convenient and efficient. From shopping and banking to accessing services and information, the internet has made it easier than ever to manage our daily tasks and responsibilities. While there are challenges and concerns associated with the convenience of the internet, the benefits of this technology as a tool for convenience cannot be overstated.

Chapter-5

Education: The internet has made education more accessible and affordable, with online courses and resources available to people around the world

The internet has revolutionized the way people access education. With online courses and resources readily available, education has become more accessible and affordable than ever before. This has opened up opportunities for people around the world to gain knowledge and skills that were previously out of reach.

Online courses have become increasingly popular in recent years, with platforms like Coursera, edX, and Udemy offering a wide range of courses in subjects ranging from computer science and engineering to business and the humanities. These courses are often taught by leading experts in their fields and are available to anyone with an internet connection. Many courses are free, while others charge a fee for a certificate or accreditation.

In addition to online courses, there are a vast number of educational resources available online. Websites like Khan Academy and TedEd offer high-quality educational videos, tutorials, and interactive lessons on a wide range of subjects. Online textbooks and research papers are also readily available, making it easier for students to access the latest research and literature in their fields of study.

The accessibility of online education has also led to the democratization of education. Students who may not have had access to traditional educational institutions due to financial or geographical barriers can now access courses and resources online. This has led to an increase in the number of people pursuing higher education and gaining skills that are valuable in the job market.

Another significant benefit of online education is its flexibility. Students can learn at their own pace and on their own schedule, allowing them to balance their studies with work or other commitments. This has made education more accessible to people who may have struggled with traditional classroom settings, such as those with disabilities or those who live in remote areas.

Despite the many benefits of online education, there are also some challenges. The lack of face-to-face interaction with instructors and peers can be a disadvantage for some students, as can the lack of structure that comes with traditional classroom settings. Additionally, not all online courses and resources are created equal, and it can be challenging for students to determine which sources are credible and reliable.

In conclusion, the internet has had a significant impact on education, making it more accessible and affordable than ever before. Online courses and resources have opened up opportunities for people around the world to gain knowledge and skills that were once out of reach. While there are challenges associated with online education, the benefits are numerous, and the trend towards online learning is likely to continue in the future.

Chapter-6

Networking: The internet has made it possible to connect with like-minded individuals and build professional and personal networks

The internet has revolutionized the way people connect with one another, enabling individuals to build professional and personal networks with like-minded individuals from around the world. Social media platforms like LinkedIn, Twitter, and Facebook have made it easier than ever before to connect with people who share similar interests or work in the same field.

One of the most significant benefits of online networking is the ability to connect with people who may be difficult to meet in person. Online networking allows individuals to reach out to people who work in different countries or who may be difficult to reach due to their busy schedules. This has made it possible for people to build networks that span the globe, enabling them to collaborate with others on projects and initiatives.

Online networking has also made it easier for individuals to find and connect with mentors and role models. By following industry leaders on social media platforms or participating in online forums and groups, individuals can gain valuable insights and advice from those who have already achieved success in their chosen fields.

In addition to professional networking, the internet has also made it possible for individuals to build personal networks with people who share similar interests or hobbies. Social media platforms like Facebook and Twitter allow individuals to connect with others who share their love of sports, music, or other interests. This has led to the formation of online communities where individuals can share ideas, experiences, and resources with one another.

One of the most significant benefits of online networking is the ability to build relationships with people over time. By engaging with others on social media platforms or participating in online forums and groups, individuals can establish meaningful connections with people who they may never have met in person. These relationships can lead to job opportunities, collaborations, and other professional and personal benefits.

While there are many benefits to online networking, there are also some risks to be aware of. It is important to be cautious when sharing personal information online and to be aware of the potential for online scams and phishing attacks. Additionally, it is essential to maintain professional standards when interacting with others online, as online interactions can impact one's reputation and career prospects.

In conclusion, the internet has made it possible to build professional and personal networks with like-minded individuals from around the world. Online networking has made it easier to connect with mentors, role models, and collaborators, and has led to the formation of online communities where individuals can share ideas and resources. While there are risks associated with online networking, the benefits are numerous, and online networking is likely to continue to grow in importance in the future.

Chapter-7

Innovation: The internet has enabled innovation in a variety of fields, from technology to healthcare, leading to new discoveries and advancements

The internet has had a profound impact on innovation, making it possible to connect people and ideas from around the world and enabling new discoveries and advancements in a wide range of fields.

One of the most significant areas where the internet has enabled innovation is technology. The internet has made it possible for software developers to collaborate with others from around the world, resulting in the creation of new and innovative products and services. This has led to advancements in areas such as artificial intelligence, virtual reality, and blockchain technology, among others.

The internet has also revolutionized the healthcare industry, enabling doctors and researchers to share information and collaborate on research projects. This has led to new discoveries and advancements in areas such as personalized medicine, telemedicine, and medical imaging, among others. In addition, the internet has made it easier for patients to access information about their health and to communicate with their doctors and other healthcare providers.

Another area where the internet has enabled innovation is in the field of education. Online learning platforms and resources have made it possible for individuals to access educational materials from around the world, enabling them to gain new skills and knowledge. This has led to new approaches to teaching and learning, including blended learning models that combine online and in-person instruction.

The internet has also enabled innovation in the field of finance, enabling the creation of new financial products and services. For example, blockchain technology has enabled the creation of cryptocurrencies such as Bitcoin, which have the potential to transform the way people conduct financial transactions. In addition, the internet has made it possible for people to access financial services and products from anywhere in the world, increasing financial inclusion and empowering people to take control of their finances.

Finally, the internet has enabled innovation in the field of communication, enabling people to connect with others from around the world in real-time. This has led to new approaches to collaboration and teamwork, enabling people to work together on projects regardless of their location. In addition, the internet has enabled new forms of communication, such as video conferencing and instant messaging, which have transformed the way people communicate with one another.

In conclusion, the internet has enabled innovation in a wide range of fields, from technology to healthcare to education and finance. The ability to connect people and ideas from around the world has led to new discoveries and advancements, transforming the way people live, work, and communicate. As the internet continues to evolve, it is likely that we will see even more innovations and advancements in the years to come.

Chapter-8

Globalization: The internet has facilitated globalization, allowing businesses and individuals to connect and collaborate on a global scale, leading to greater economic growth and cultural exchange

The internet has had a significant impact on globalization, making it possible for businesses and individuals to connect and collaborate with each other on a global scale. This has led to greater economic growth and cultural exchange, enabling people to share ideas and resources from around the world.

One of the most significant ways that the internet has facilitated globalization is by making it easier for businesses to connect with customers and partners from around the world. E-commerce platforms like Amazon and Alibaba have made it possible for businesses to sell their products to customers in other countries, enabling them to tap into new markets and grow their customer base. The internet has also made it possible for businesses to collaborate with partners from around the world, enabling them to share knowledge and resources and to create new products and services.

The internet has also facilitated greater cultural exchange, enabling people to connect with others from around the world and to learn about different cultures and ways of life. Social media platforms like Facebook and Twitter have made it possible for people to share their experiences and ideas with others, enabling them to build relationships and to learn from one another. In addition, online learning platforms and resources have made it possible for people to access educational materials from around the world, enabling them to gain new skills and knowledge.

The internet has also enabled greater economic growth, enabling businesses to access new markets and to tap into new sources of talent and resources. This has led to greater competition and innovation, as businesses strive to stay ahead of their competitors and to create new products and services that meet the needs of customers around the world. In addition, the internet has enabled greater collaboration and teamwork, enabling businesses to work together on projects regardless of their location.

However, there are also challenges associated with globalization, including concerns about the impact on local economies and the environment. Some people argue that globalization has led to the loss of jobs and the exploitation of workers in developing countries. Others argue that globalization has contributed to environmental problems such as climate change and deforestation.

In conclusion, the internet has facilitated globalization, enabling businesses and individuals to connect and collaborate with each other on a global scale. This has led to greater economic growth and cultural exchange, enabling people to share ideas and resources from around the world. While there are challenges associated with globalization, the benefits are numerous, and the internet is likely to continue to play a significant role in driving globalization in the future.

www.ingramcontent.com/pod-product-compliance
Lightning Source LLC
Chambersburg PA
CBHW040350220526
45473CB00009B/2843